The High Weald Dairy Cookbook

Classic Kent and Sussex Recipes Updated

First published in paperback by
Michael Terence Publishing in 2025
www.mtp.agency

ISBN 9781805880233

Cover image
courtesy of Lyn Funnell

Michael Terence
Publishing

I'm Not a Trained Chef – I'm an Enthusiastic Foodie

My favourite recipes are Peasant recipes; simple, delicious, unpretentious and made with fresh ingredients.

I love discovering a new recipe, and I often add my own twist.

These recipes have been carefully checked and re-checked for mistakes. So if you see 6 tablespoons of salt in a dessert instead of sugar, anyone above idiot level should realise that it's wrong!

No, there aren't any mistakes like that! I'm joking.

Sir Simon Rattle, the great Conductor, said that when he was training, six finalists had to conduct an orchestra, and each time the tune sounded completely different.

My point is, if six of you prepare the same recipe, they will all turn out different. You will use ingredients from different sources, supermarkets, countries, farmers markets, etc.

All ovens are different. If I say Cook in the oven for an hour, and it starts to turn black after 45 minutes, take it out!

When the amazing Elizabeth David was collecting Italian recipes, she was constantly frustrated as they would say Add a handful of flour. They cooked instinctively, not by recipes.

People often didn't have kitchen scales. They couldn't afford them.

I asked my Mum for her Yorkshire Pudding recipe and she said, 'You mix eggs, flour, milk and water.'

'Yes, but how much?' I asked.

And she shrugged. 'I don't know. I just mix it until it's right.'

My recipes are as accurate as I could make them. But don't just follow them to the letter. Taste your food as you go along.

Many of the recipes can be adapted. For instance, my Apple Cheesecake recipe; you could add some blackberries, or a dash of mixed spice or cinnamon. It's up to you.

And get to know your herbs. They can really add something subtle to your dish.

Remember, in cookery you can add but you can't subtract!

But the main thing is, enjoy yourself. Cookery and eating are two of the greatest pleasures in life.

Well I think so!

– Lyn –

Contents

Introduction

High Weald Dairy began in the late 1980s when a flock of 250 dairy sheep were established by Mark and his parents on the small farm at Duddleswell on the Ashdown Forest, in the High Weald of Sussex.

Sheep had been milked all over Europe since millennia, but in the UK it has not been such a common occurrence. Sheep milk is highly nutritious, with up to twice the goodness of cow milk and with a creamy, moreish sweet flavour. Due to the high digestibility of sheep milk, initially it was bottled and sold to customers who were intolerant to cow milk. Gradually over the next few years a range of sheep milk yogurts and cheeses were developed and supplied to farm shops and delicatessens.

These included Halloumi, Ricotta, Medita (Feta style) Duddleswell hard cheese, and Sussex Slipcote soft cheese. Other local dairy sheep farmers also supplied Sheep milk to keep up with the growing demand for sheep milk dairy products.

It was in 2003 that the cheese production moved to Tremains Farm in Horsted Keynes, where a redundant grain store was converted into a modern cheese dairy. The farm was also milking 200 organic cows and gradually the organic cow milk cheese range expanded to include to include Saint Giles, Ashdown Forester, and the popular Brighton Blue.

An enthusiastic cheesemaking team now craft the cheese range alongside Mark and his wife Sarah, with cheeses supplied to independent shops and restaurants throughout the south east. The Dairy also has a popular online presence for Cheese Hampers and Gifts.

In addition to their thriving business in the south east, Mark and Sarah's cheese has gained a reputation for exceptional quality, winning numerous awards at both national and international cheese competitions. Their dedication to traditional cheesemaking techniques blended with modern innovations has set them apart in the artisanal cheese community.

The couple also places a strong emphasis on sustainability and animal welfare, ensuring that their production practices are environmentally friendly and milk suppliers are committed to animal welfare. This commitment is reflected in the superior quality of their cheese, which boasts rich, complex flavours and a distinctive character.

As their business continues to grow, Mark and Sarah remain deeply connected to their local community, often hosting farm tours and cheesemaking workshops to share their passion and knowledge with others. Their story is one of resilience, innovation, and a profound love for cheese making, true pioneers in the world of British cheese.

ARTISAN CHEESE DISHES

Created for the Earl of Sandwich

– A Tradition Since the 1700s –

Tradition says that in 1762 John Montague, the 4th Earl of Sandwich was the first person to order a sandwich.

The first story says that he was engrossed in a gambling game and didn't want to stop to eat, so he asked a valet to prepare some roast beef between two lightly toasted slices of bread.

The second version is that he was busy with his Naval duties and couldn't leave his desk.

Both versions say that he didn't want to get his fingers greasy.

I lean towards the gambling version as the sandwich rapidly became popular and people would order 'The same as Sandwich' so I think that he was observed eating his meal.

But what is the connection with the town of Sandwich in Kent?

The first Earl, Edward Montague, was in Sandwich because his fleet of ships was waiting there to bring back Charles II to England in 1660. So he was made the Earl of Sandwich.

The 4th Earl of Sandwich was a colourful character. He was a Member of the notorious Hellfire Club, and took part in drunken orgies and lots of other dark pastimes.

He had as many as 9 children with his mistress, Martha Ray. But he was also a very active politician.

Captain James Cook named the Sandwich Islands (which became Hawaii) after the 4th Earl, who was his financial Patron.

Here is my version of the original Sandwich. I've researched it and made it as authentic as I can.

But even if it's not the completely original Sandwich, it's delicious!

The Georgians didn't have snacks, although they would have bowls of nibbles and sweetmeats around them all day. So the Earl's sandwich would have been large, well-filled, and a substitute for a meal. I don't think the valet would have just stuck some meat between two slices of bread. I think he would have made the sandwich as attractive and as filling to eat as he could.

Spread 2 large thick slices of bread with butter. I used sourdough bread.

Butter was well-known in Georgian times.

Next, spread a layer of chutney or relish over the bread.

Pickles, chutneys and relishes had been around at least since the 1600s. I used my home-made Pumpkin Chutney.

Add 1 or 2 slices of corned beef.

The Earl would probably have been given salt beef as there was no refrigeration to preserve the meat. Corned beef is salt beef with gelatine added.

Top with a flavoursome cheese.

I used Organic Sussex Velvet, a semi-soft mature cheese, made in High Weald Dairy in Horsted Keynes. The cheese melted perfectly.

Toast the sandwich on both sides until light golden and the cheese has just begun to melt.

The Earl's sandwich would have been toasted on the fire as George Forman hadn't invented his grill then! If you don't own a sandwich grill, toast it under the grill on the cooker.

Cut the sandwich in half and make sure the inside isn't too hot to eat – and you probably won't get greasy fingers!

Posh Sandwiches

– From the Earl of Sandwich –

The Earl of Sandwich was the Kentish person who made the sandwich popular.

It was said that he ate them while he was playing cards at the gambling table.

Very soon, in the late 1700s, sandwiches became dainty and attractive. And tea-time became an additional meal to keep hunger at bay before dinner.

The Queen and the Queen Mother had tea every afternoon between 3 and 5 o'clock.

Crusts were cut off and the sandwiches were cut into triangles.

One of their favourites was cucumber sandwiches.

Try their recipe. The addition of a tiny amount of mint adds a nice, subtle flavour.

1 thin cucumber

8 slices brown bread, sliced

8 slices white bread, sliced

4oz fresh unsalted butter

1-2 tsp finely chopped fresh mint

Salt and pepper

2oz cream cheese

Peel cucumber and slice into thin rounds. Salt rounds lightly and place in colander for 15 minutes to drain. Press to release water, and pat dry with paper towels.

Spread the sliced bread with softened butter. Put 2 layers of cucumber slices on bottom slice, sprinkle with finely chopped mint, salt and pepper to taste, and top with another buttered slice. Press lightly with your hand.

Cut all crusts off with a sharp knife, making sure that you don't break the ends. But save the crusts. Cut sandwiches in half diagonally and then again into quarters.

Serve in alternate rows of brown and white bread sandwiches, points facing up.

Sandwiches can also be cut into fingers.

You can add cream cheese to the fillings.

Other fillings are egg mayonnaise, ham, smoked salmon or cheese.

Display the sandwiches attractively. Tiny cakes, and scones with clotted cream and jam are also popular.

Remember that I suggested you save the crusts?

Make your own Cheese Straws

Roll the crusts in butter and then grated cheese, pushing down firmly, and bake them in the oven until the cheese melts, turning over after a few minutes.

Crunchy and delicious!

Sussex Churdles

– Oggy Oggy Oggy! Oi Oi Oi! –

Oggy Oggy Oggy! Oi Oi Oi!

This is a chant often shouted out during parades, such as the Sussex Bonfire Parades which take place in November each year.

Someone in the Procession will suddenly shout out Oggy Oggy Oggy! And the crowd will obediently shout back, Oi Oi Oi!

It's usually repeated twice more.

But what does it mean, I hear you asking.

Oggy was the original name of Cornish Pasties. It was a corruption of Hogan.

Apparently the Cornish wives used to shout Oggy Oggy Oggy! when their fresh-baked pasties were ready. And their husbands, usually down the tin mines, would shout back, Oi Oi Oi! to let their wives know that they'd heard them.

The same cry is used today by the Devenport Gun team when they are returning from the Royal Tournament to their Plymouth Naval Base. They have a Cornish Pasty as a symbol.

In the 1970s the Welsh comedian Max Boyce turned it into a chant, and it's been popular in football stadiums ever since.

The Sussex version of the Cornish Pasty is the Sussex Churdle. It's supposed to have originated in Chichester and it possibly dates back to the 17th Century.

To churd meant to turn over. But as the Cornish Pasty is a circle folded in half, the Sussex version is pulled up to the centre and squeezed shut, like a purse.

To make 4 Churdles

1 large onion, chopped

1lb lambs liver, chopped

2oz bacon, chopped

1 tablespoon fresh sage, optional
You could use parsley instead or as well

1 apple, peeled, cored and chopped

salt and pepper

1oz butter, or olive oil
I don't think that olive oil would have been available in the 17th Century. They would probably have used lard

2oz breadcrumbs

4oz Cheddar cheese, grated
I used a local cheese from the High Weald Dairy

10oz rough-puff pastry

The ready-made Supermarket pastry is really good now, and it's Vegan. You can use shortcrust pastry instead

Egg to wash. I used milk

Roll the pastry into four 7-inch circles. I use a soup bowl for this and cut around it.

Soften the chopped onion in the butter or oil, add the bacon and liver and cook for a couple of minutes until slightly browned. Add the apple, herbs if used, and seasoning and cook until heated through, stirring it regularly.

Divide the mixture into piles in the centre of each pastry circle and top with grated cheese and breadcrumbs.

Brush the edges with egg or milk to help the churdle to stick together, and use both hands to gather the pastry around to form a purse shape, pushing the filling down and squeezing the edges firmly together at the top.

Brush with egg or milk and bake upside-down for 10 minutes to avoid the top splitting open. Then turn them right way up and bake for a further 15-20 minutes or until crisp and golden.

Careful when biting into it as the inside will be very hot!

Serve with chips and beans, or with a side salad.

Potato Upside-down Tart

– With Little Sussex cheese –

This is an unusual tart but well worth the effort!

Just build up the layers.

Approx. 10 cherry tomatoes, cut in half
Do use these, as larger tomatoes sliced
make too much liquid

Approx. 2 tbsp olive oil to cover the pan

Seasoning

Approx. 4 large potatoes, or a dozen small potatoes, boiled until soft but not breaking up

1 large red onion, finely chopped

3 tbsp sugar

2 tsp butter or margarine

Approx. 5oz cheese
I used 2 Little Sussex cheeses, sliced

1 roll of prepared shortcrust or puff pastry

Preheat the oven to 400F, 200C, gas mark 6.

Boil the potatoes until just soft. Drain.

Heat the olive oil in a frying-pan.

Saute the onions slowly until soft.

Add the tomatoes, gently turning them over after a minute.

Put the pan aside.

Cook the butter and sugar in a pan, stirring until it just turns a caramel colour.

Tip it into a 9-inch tin or flan dish, spreading it over the bottom.

Slice the potatoes about ½-inch thick, cutting off the ends, and place them fitted together to cover the bottom of the dish.

Fit the tomatoes and onion in the gaps between the potatoes, placing the tomatoes skin side down, gently pressing them down.

Cut the cheese thinly and lay the slices on top of the potato slices.

Lay the pastry over the dish, cutting off the surplus pastry and tucking the edges underneath and pressing them down to neaten them.

Bake the tart for 25 minutes, then turn the heat down to 300F, 250C, gas mark 2 and bake for a further 15 minutes until it's a dark, golden colour and obviously cooked.

Remove from the oven and let it stand for 5 minutes to set.

Gently slip a knife round the edge to loosen it.

Invert a large plate on top of the tart, then carefully but quickly turn the tart upside down, then lift off the plate.

The tart should have dropped out and will show off its pattern.

Let it cool slightly before serving.

Serve it with a salad, or take it on a picnic.

Kentish Broccoli and Blue Cheese Flan

– Fresh From Kent: The Broccoli County –

Kent is one of the biggest broccoli producers in the UK.

If possible, use one of our local cheeses for this recipe. I've used the award-winning Brighton Blue, made by High Weald Dairy in Sussex. It has a delicious tangy flavour, perfect for this recipe.

This is different to a normal quiche as the cheese is used in slices, not grated.

I was eager to try it!

225g/8oz broccoli florets
175g/6oz plain flour
75g/3oz butter or margarine
Seasoning
175g/6oz thinly sliced blue cheese
3 eggs, beaten
300ml/½ pint milk, or milk and single cream
1 medium onion, finely chopped
Chives (optional)
I didn't use any

Pre-heat the oven to 200C/400F/gas mark 6. Grease a flan dish approx. 25cm/10in diameter.

Mix the flour with the butter and a pinch of salt. Rub until it resembles fine breadcrumbs, then add 2-3 tablespoons cold water to form a firm dough.

NB. I bought a roll of ready-made pastry from the supermarket. It was as good as home-made pastry.

Roll out the pastry and use it to line the greased flan dish.

Place a piece of greaseproof paper on the pastry and fill it with baking beans.

NB. I pricked the pastry all over with a fork, which does the same job; stops the pastry rising.

Bake it for 10 minutes, then remove the beans and paper (if used) and bake for a further 5 minutes to dry the base.

Remove from the oven and reduce the heat to 190C/275F/gas mark 5.

The Baked Pastry and Brighton Blue Cheese

While the pastry is cooking, boil the broccoli in a little water for approx. 2 minutes. Drain and slice lengthways into pieces.

Mix the eggs and milk together. Add the chopped onion and chives, if using. Season lightly. The cheese will already have salt in it.

Lay the slices of cheese on the bottom of the cooled flan case, adding any cheese crumbs.

Neatly spread the broccoli florets on top of the cheese, then pour over the egg, cheese and onion mixture.

Ready for The Oven

Bake in the oven for 40-45 minutes until the top of the flan is slightly browned then take it out of the oven. The flan will still wobble slightly, but it will carry on cooking and firm up.

I stood the flan in a flat baking tin to catch any spillage, but there wasn't any.

This shouldn't be eaten hot. Leave it to cool a bit and firm up. Or eat it cold with a salad, or a jacket potato, or chips.

You could also pack it in a plastic box and take it on a picnic.

And the results? Absolutely delicious! The Brighton Blue cheese comes through and gives a lovely tangy flavour to the dish.

I'll definitely be making it again.

Sussex Christmas Cranberry Cheese Quiche

– A Post-Christmas Treasure –

This is an ideal post-Christmas recipe when you're fed up with large meals and you have lots of food left over, like cheese, milk, cream, Cranberry Sauce and salad to serve with it.

I used shop-bought shortcrust pastry, but of course you can make your own if you want to.

Shortcrust pastry for the base

Knob of butter or marge

1 small or ½ a large red onion, finely chopped

150g Sussex Marble Cranberry Cheese

3 eggs

5ml combined milk and cream

1 tbsp cranberry sauce

Roll out the pastry to fit the flan dish of your choice. Press it well into the edges.

I roll the pastry thinner than it is in the packet and it goes much further.

Gently fry the onion in the melted butter until it's soft.

Stir the eggs into the milk and cream.

Add the cranberry sauce and mix in well.

Grate half the packet of cheese and add to the mixture. Lay any large bits that haven't grated into the flan case.

Slice half the packet of cheese and spread the slices over the bottom of the pastry.

Spread the onion on the top.

Tip in the egg mixture.

Bake in the oven at 180C for about half an hour, until the top is just beginning to turn golden.

Serve with a salad, jacket potato or chips, depending on how hungry you're feeling!

Golden Cheesy Bread Balls

– Polpetti di Pane –

These are called Polpetti di Pane in Italian, where they're very popular.

Here's a recipe giving them a Sussex flavour.

Don't throw your leftover bread away! Make these tasty Golden Cheesy Bread Balls.

These are cheap to make and delicious as a snack, or a main meal with chips, beans, or a salad.

You don't need to be exact with the ingredients. A small difference won't do any harm.

120g stale bread, with crusts on

Water to soak

60-70g grated hard cheese
Don't use Cheddar as it's too oily. I used Sister Sarah, a Goats Cheese from the High Weald Dairy in Sussex

3 eggs, beaten

2 tbsp chopped parsley

1 chopped garlic clove (optional)

Black pepper
Don't add salt as the cheese will be salty enough

Vegetable oil

Roughly break the bread into a bowl.

Cover with cold water, press down and leave for approx. ½ hour, occasionally breaking the bread up with your hands.

Squeeze out as much water as you can. Add the other ingredients. Mix well.

Heat some oil in a pan. When it's hot, form small balls of the mixture in your hand, squeezing out any liquid.

Drop them gently into the oil. Fry until golden, turning them over and frying the other side.

Drain on kitchen paper and serve while hot or warm.

They will be crunchy on the outside and soft and cheesy inside.

Peasant food at its best!

Bread Tarts

- A Great Bread Recipe -

Here is another great recipe, using bread.

The filling is your choice. You could use roast or stewed vegetables, or a sweet filling, like jam.

12 slices of bread, or as many as you want to use

Butter or margarine

For the filling:

> ½ an onion and a tomato, finely chopped fried in oil until soft
>
> 3 eggs, lightly beaten
>
> 300ml/14floz milk
>
> 85g/3oz grated cheese
> I used High Weald Dairy's Ricotta Salata, made with cow and sheep whey

Either cut off the crusts, making a square shape or use a round cutter to cut out circles.

Using a rolling pin, roll out the slices one at a time, turning them over and rolling the other side, to flatten them. Make sure you keep their shape.

Butter one side and place them, butter side down, in muffin or bun tins. Press them down.

I added a base of stewed onion and tomato in the squares.

Beat the eggs, milk and cheese together.

Lightly season but go easy on the salt as the cheese will be slightly salty.

Spoon the milk mixture over the bread cases, leaving room for them to expand.

Bake at 190C/375F/gas mark 5, for 25-30 minutes.

Sussex Cauliflower Cheese Patties

– Quick and Delicious –

Light but filling, these tasty cauliflower patties are very easy to make. You just blitz the ingredients in a food processor, then spoon them onto a baking tray.

They're a useful recipe for when you don't feel like spending ages preparing a meal, or eating much. And they're absolutely delicious!

Use a fairly strong cheese as the cauliflower has a distinctive flavour.

Oil, for greasing the tray

Approx. ½ a cauliflower

A small piece of onion

1 slice of bread

1 egg

50g grated cheese and extra for the topping
I used High Weald Dairy's Brighton Blue

Seasoning
Go easy on the salt as the cheese is slightly salty

Heat the oven to 180C/gas mark 4 and grease a flat baking tray.

Cook the cauliflower until it's just soft. Drain it.

Blitz the bread in a food processor until it's crumbs.

Then add the other ingredients and blitz until well-mixed.

It's easier to handle if you leave it in the fridge for an hour or more.

Scoop up a dessert spoonful and gently pat it into a circle, then turn the spoon over and drop the patty on the baking tray, flattening it slightly.

Bake for about 20 minutes until they're golden and risen.

Turn the oven off. Remove from the oven and sprinkle some grated cheese on the top. Put them back in the oven and leave for a few minutes until the cheese melts.

I served them with a salad, but you could serve them with chips, or boiled potatoes.

Sussex Brussels Sprout Crumble

– Sprout Haters, Be Converted! –

I must admit that the British aren't the greatest vegetable cooks, although we grow a large selection of really flavoursome vegetables.

Our generation was raised on over-boiled, tasteless vegetables, served with a few slices of meat and covered with gravy.

Post-war wives cooked what their mothers had cooked during the war, usually with no variations or imagination at all.

Even now, to a lot of the older generation 'size does matter'. As long as the plate is piled high with soggy vegetables or frozen chips, they think they're getting value-for-money.

But people are beginning to rebel as they travel abroad or visit restaurants and discover how versatile the humble vegetable can be. And vegetarians and vegans expect a variety to their diet.

So all you Sprout Haters, do try this dish and enjoy the sweet baby cabbages cooked like this!

Serves 4 as a side dish or 2-3 as a meal

You really don't need to worry about exact measurements. Rely on your tastebuds.

2oz melted butter or margarine, or oil

1 onion, chopped

250g/½lb Brussels sprouts, chopped
This might not seem like a lot, but it is when they're chopped

Seasoning

For the white sauce:

2oz melted butter or marge

1 heaped tbsp flour

½ pt milk and extra to thin down the sauce

3oz Duddleswell cheese

2oz Brighton Blue cheese
You can use any cheese you like, but don't use strong cheese that overpowers the dish

Seasoning

For the crumble:

3 slices of fresh bread, blitzed to crumbs

2oz Duddleswell cheese, added to the crumbs and blitzed

Melt the butter. Gently cook the onion for a couple of minutes.

Add the sprouts. Mix and heat through.

Tip into a baking dish. Season.

Make Lyn's All-in-One White Sauce

Melt the butter. Add the flour and milk and stir until smooth and thickening.

Add the cheeses. Taste. Add more cheese if you like.

Add seasoning.

If the sauce gets very thick, add more milk or milk and cream, to thin down to a thick pouring consistency.

Pour on top of the sprouts and mix well.

Top with the crumble mix.

Bake in the oven at approx. 180C for 20-30 minutes until crispy and golden.

Serve on its own or as a side dish with a main meal.

NB You don't have to tell anyone the recipe until they've tried it and said how tasty it is!

HALLOUMI RECIPES

High Weald Halloumi Hotpot

– With a Meaty Taste –

Approx. 4oz/120g Halloumi, cut into small cubes
Oil, to line pan
1 onion, finely chopped
Approx. 6 mushrooms, chopped
2 potatoes, 1 finely chopped, 1 sliced

1 carrot, sliced

1 sprig of parsley, finely chopped

Breadcrumbs to cover potatoes

Seasoning

50g grated cheese and extra for the topping
I used High Weald Dairy's Brighton Blue

Dry fry the Halloumi in a pan, turning it, until each side is golden.

Take it out of the pan and transfer to a dish.

Add oil to the pan. Fry the chopped onion.

Add the mushrooms, chopped potato, carrot, parsley and seasoning.

Cook for a minute until lightly browned, stirring.

Tip it all into an oven dish and add the Halloumi. Go easy on the salt as the cheese is slightly salty.

Layer the slices of potato neatly over the top. Add a layer of breadcrumbs and grated cheese.

Cover with water.

Cook in a slow oven for an hour or until the potatoes are soft and golden.

You can leave the dish in the oven for longer, until you're ready to serve it.

The Halloumi will taste like meat. If you have guests, they won't realise that they're eating a vegetarian dish.

Squash and Halloumi Risotto

– Simple and Tasty –

This is a very simple dish, but delicious!
So good that I won a Nationwide competition with it.

All ingredients are approximate.
Keep tasting while you're cooking.

I used Sussex Halloumi from the High Weald Dairy
Olive oil

8oz/175g approx. Halloumi, cubed

1 onion, chopped

8oz/175g squash, cubed

8oz/175g Arborio rice
(long-grain will do, but stir it more often)

Vegetable stock
(A stock cube will do)

Chopped parsley

Seasoning

Dry-fry the Halloumi in a large frying-pan for about 2 minutes until beginning to go brown. Remove from pan.

Add some olive oil to the pan; enough to cover the base.

Add the onion and fry slowly until transparent

Add the squash, rice, parsley, the Halloumi and enough vegetable stock to cover the ingredients. Stir and season.

You can add a few chopped mushrooms if you like.

Simmer for about half an hour. Stir regularly. Add more stock as it's absorbed.

The rice should become creamy.

Taste. Adjust the seasoning.

Leave to stand for about 5 minutes to absorb the stock.

Serve with more parsley sprinkled on top.

Halloumi Chips

– A Snack or a Meal –

The Halloumi keeps its shape during cooking. Do try this recipe and watch how quickly they get eaten!

1 tbsp plain flour

1 level tsp curry powder

Approx. 4oz/120g Halloumi

Cooking oil

Mix the flour and curry powder in a plastic bag without holes.

Cut the Halloumi into chunky chips. Place them into the flour mix and shake the bag until they're well-coated.

Fry them until golden, for about 5 minutes.

Serve as a snack, or with a salad.

ASSORTED

RECIPES

Chiddingly Hotpot

– An Old Sussex Recipe –

This is a recipe from an old cookbook, Sussex Recipes, published in 1937.

Approx.1lb of beef, sliced
1lb onions, chopped
8oz celery, chopped
8oz olives, chopped
1lb potatoes, sliced
Cloves

Mixed spice

Tarragon vinegar

Place a layer of onions on the bottom of a large casserole dish, with some of the olives and celery.

Put thin slices of beef on top and sprinkle with a little spice and vinegar.

Add slices of potato over the meat, with some more celery and olives.

Repeat until all the ingredients are used up.

Pour enough water into the casserole to nearly cover.

Cook in a low oven for 3-4 hours.

The vinegar renders salt unnecessary.

The fun of cooking is using what you have available, and sometimes you have to change the ingredients…

I didn't have any beef so I used pork. But you could use lamb or chicken. They would work just as well.

I like to use the celery leaves as I think they add a lovely flavour.

The only olives I had were in a tin and stuffed with chorizo. I just chopped them in half and I didn't use 8oz. They added a delicious flavour.

I didn't have any tarragon vinegar but I had cider vinegar, which worked perfectly with the pork.

You don't need cloves as they're included in mixed spice.

Half the cooking time is plenty, if the potato slices have gone soft when you poke them with a fork.

But the casserole will stay in the oven for longer on a low heat if you're not ready to serve it.

Sussex Bacon Roly Poly

– With Oven-Baked Suet –

This is another old Sussex recipe.

It's different to usual suet recipes as it's baked in the oven, not steamed.

8oz self-raising flour

A pinch of salt

4oz shredded suet

7-8 tbsp cold water

12oz bacon rashers, cut small

1 onion, chopped

Fresh or dried sage, chopped

Black pepper

Beaten egg, or milk, to glaze

Sift flour and salt into a bowl. Add suet and mix with water to a soft but not sticky dough.

Add a drop more water if you need to.

Knead to a ball, then using a floured board, roll it out thinly.

Cover generously with bacon and onion, and mix in the sage and pepper.

Roll up into a long roll, sealing the edge and the sides with milk.

Glaze with the egg or milk (optional.)

Bake near the top of an oven, 200C/400F/gas mark 6 for 30-40 minutes, until crusty and golden.

I didn't have any sage so I used thyme.

I laid the pastry on top of oiled tinfoil and I used the foil to help with the rolling up.

I baked it at a cooler temperature, for a longer time, 1 hour, peeling back the foil for the last 20 minutes, to keep the pastry moister and not too crusty.

Serve with mashed potatoes and vegetables of your choice.

Serve with a white parsley sauce or gravy.

Traditional Sussex Bacon Pudding

– Economical and Delicious –

I was a bit worried about this recipe as it had no liquid addition, or nothing juicy like tomatoes.

But when it's been steamed, the ingredients are soft, so it does work well.

Approx. 125g/4oz plain flour

1½ tsp baking powder

50g/2oz suet

1 egg

Milk, if necessary

1 onion, finely chopped

Bacon, chopped.
I had some leftover bacon pieces which I cut up with kitchen scissors

1 tsp mixed herbs

Seasoning

I didn't think the basin was full enough, so I added a few chopped potato skins and some leftover boiled potatoes, chopped

Mix the pastry ingredients. Add a few drops of milk if it's too dry.

Roll out, then cut a triangle for the lid.

Line a well-greased 1pt basin, repairing any gaps.

Place all the ingredients into the basin.

Place the lid on the top, firmly pressing the edge shut.

Cover the top with greaseproof paper, then cover the whole basin with tinfoil.

Place in a saucepan filled about a third with boiling water.

The recipe says steam for 1½ hours, but I didn't think that was long enough, so I steamed it for 2½ hours.

Check regularly to make sure the water doesn't dry up. Top up if necessary.

Remove foil and greaseproof, then using a knife, run it around the edge to loosen the pastry. Place a dish on top and tip the basin upside-down.

The pudding should drop out in one piece.

I served it with baked beans.

It's not a pretty dish, but it's a traditional, economical delicious meal!

Sussex Corned Beef and Onion Pie

– Basic and Traditional –

This is a basic but delicious traditional Sussex pie.

The corned beef melts into the vegetables to create a bubble and squeak-type pie filling.

Use any type of pastry topping that you fancy.

The original recipe uses a shortcrust pastry, but I used puff pastry as I had some available.

You don't need to be exact with your measurements.
A slight deviation does no harm.

340g/12oz Corned Beef

50g/2oz butter or margarine

1 tbsp olive oil

300g/11oz potatoes, diced

2 medium carrots

2 celery sticks
I like cooking with the celery leaves as I prefer their flavour

2-3 tbsp tomato Ketchup

Black pepper

Only add salt if it's needed as the corned beef is quite salty

I added a shake of Worcestershire Sauce

Taste the mixture and if you want to add any extra tomato sauce, Worcestershire Sauce, a drop of water or salt, do so.

For the filling, melt the butter and oil in a pan.

Add the onion, potatoes, carrots and celery.

Cook over a low heat, stirring regularly until the vegetables soften.

Do spend time on this so the potatoes soften.

Add more oil if necessary, and a small amount of water if the vegetables begin to stick.

Stir in the ketchup, to taste.

Crumble in the corned beef and stir until heated through.

Add the black pepper.

Tip into a baking dish and top with the pastry.

Bake for approx. 40 minutes until the pastry is golden and the filling is hot.

Stuffed Sussex Pumpkin and Filo Tubes

– Overwhelmed with Pumpkins –

I've got enough Sussex pumpkins to last me through to Easter. But they can become rather boring. So try this unusual recipe that I've created.

It's simple to make. I'm really proud of it!

I used an orange-coloured pumpkin.

The day before:

Cut your pumpkin open and remove the seeds and the stringy bits.

Then slice the pumpkin into about 6 or 8 portions, depending on the size of your pumpkin.

Using a mandolin or a very sharp knife, cut thin slices. You can leave the peel on as it softens when cooked.

Marinate the slices in a mixture of 1 tbsp sugar, and 1 part vinegar to 2 parts water. Stir to dissolve the sugar.

Leave the slices overnight or longer so they become flexible and they won't break when you roll them.

For the next day:

Approx. 4oz butter or marge

Small red onion, chopped

4 largish mushrooms, chopped

1 tbsp curry powder

1 tbsp apricot jam

Seasoning

Herbs of your choice, dried or fresh, chopped
I used rosemary, thyme and sage

A splash of red wine

Double cream, to cover the ingredients

Packet of rolled filo pastry

Pumpkin slices, drained

Melt approx. 2oz of the butter in a saucepan.

Add the onion and gently cook for about a minute.

Add all the other ingredients except the pumpkin slices and cook slowly, stirring until the sauce has reduced and thickened.

Melt the rest of the butter.

Open out the filo sheets and brush the top one with butter.

Lay out two of the pumpkin slices, overlapping and leaving edges around them so the mixture doesn't leak.

Cut to the end of the filo sheet.

Spoon some of the mixture on top of the pumpkin. Tuck in the pastry edges each side of the filling and roll it up, pressing in the mixture as you roll. Repeat until all the filling's used up.

Lay the tubes, open side down, in a tray. Brush the rest of the melted butter over the tops.

Bake for approx. 15 minutes, until they're crispy and golden.

Serve as nibblies or as part of a main meal.

I served them with matchstick potatoes and a mixed salad.

If you have any left, they're equally delicious the next day when they're cold. Cut them into 4 and serve as canapes.

Kentish Twice Laid Fishcakes

– A Tasty Local Recipe –

There are still fishing boats of different sizes right along the Kent and Sussex coast. Fishing has always been an important industry around the British coast. Most of them operate from a harbour, but some of them are beached and have to be towed into the water, mainly in Deal, Hythe, Dungeness and Hastings.

The fishing industry has sadly declined nowadays, but there are still quite a lot of licenced boats, which is good to know, as you can't beat the taste of freshly-caught fish!

I go to Hastings several times a year and I buy my fish straight off the beach.

Do try this recipe as it's easy to prepare, and it makes the fish go a long way.

It's called Twice Laid Fishcakes because it includes chopped hard-boiled eggs.

My advice is, keep your board and your hands well-floured, and handle the fishcakes as little as possible as they are quite delicate.

Approx. 12oz white fish
It was originally made with cod. I used huss, but any filleted white fish will do

½ pt milk, enough to cover the fish

12oz cooked, mashed potatoes

A knob of butter

2 hard-boiled eggs

1 egg, beaten

Breadcrumbs

Seasoning

Place the fish in a saucepan, cover with milk and simmer gently for around 6 minutes, until the flesh is breaking up.

Grease a baking tray. Heat the oven to 190C/375F/gas mark 5.

Gently lift the fish out of the pan, reserving the milk.

I easily scraped the flesh of the huss off the long, hard bone.

Mix the fish and potatoes together, adding a knob of butter, and a little milk to help to bind it together.

I used a hand mixer, which made it light and creamy.

Season it to taste.

Chop the two hard-boiled eggs into small pieces and gently stir them into the fish mixture.

Thickly cover your board and hands with flour and, using a spoon, scoop out some of the mixture, gently roll them into balls, then dip them with the beaten egg and roll them in the breadcrumbs.

Place the balls on the baking tray and bake in the oven for 20 minutes until they are golden and crisp on the outside.

They will still be soft inside.

The balls will flatten in the oven as they cook.

I served mine with straw potatoes and samphire. But a salad would be just as tasty!

Samphire is a salty plant that grows on the coast. I buy some when I go to Hastings.

I gently heat it in water and serve it with fish.

Sussex Squid Stew

– Not Pretty but Flavoursome –

Cephalopods, which include octopus squid and cuttlefish, aren't just caught in the Mediterranean. They are caught all along the Kent and Sussex coast as well. They're cheap and delicious, but a lot of people won't touch them.

No, they're not the prettiest of seafood, and they're messy to clean. But your fishmonger will often clean them for you.

I bought a large fresh squid on Hastings seafront from one of the little shacks on the beach.

Although it was extra work for me, I wanted to clean it myself to rescue the ink sac, which adds a nice flavour to the sauce.

You can read instructions online on how to clean your squid. It's easy.

After I'd skinned it, I turned it inside-out and gently pulled out and put aside the ink sac, then I rinsed it under the tap. Then, using kitchen scissors, I cut the white meat into small squares.

Approx. 4 tbsp olive oil

4 mixed red, yellow and green peppers
I thought this was too much, so I just used half a large yellow pepper

1 red onion, chopped

100g chorizo
I can't stand chorizo, but I had some Serrano ham so I chopped that up. But bacon would do

½ tsp chilli flakes
or use a dash of chilli sauce

Thyme, to taste

Parsley, fresh or dried

1 bay leaf

4 garlic cloves, chopped

500ml red wine vinegar
I didn't have any, so I used malt vinegar, which added a nice tang

25g caster sugar
This seemed pointless, so I used granulated

500ml passata
I didn't have any, so I used a tin of chopped tomatoes

400g squid
I don't know what mine weighed, but it was a whole squid

400g butter beans, drained
This is a clever addition that I wouldn't have thought of using

Seasoning

Heat the oil in a large saucepan.

Gently fry the onion, pepper until soft.

Add the other ingredients, including the squid and the ink and add some water.

Bring to the boil, stirring regularly. Cover with a lid.

The ink will burst and turn the sauce black.

Simmer for approx. 1 hour.

If necessary, you can cook it for longer. But check that it doesn't burn. Top up with water if necessary.

Serve it with crusty bread or rice.

I used jasmine rice because it's pure white and looked good with the black sauce.

Hummus

– Made from "Anything" –

We had some cooked food left over from our Sunday dinner; some sugar snap peas, marrow and turnip. All bought from local producers and kept in the freezer.

I'd heard that you can turn almost anything into hummus; carrots, broad beans, beetroot, chickpeas, peppers, chestnuts, sweet potatoes and more. But I'd never tried any variations of the traditional dish.

Most of them have a pulse or bean base, like chickpeas or broad beans. I had peas, including their pods.

A selection of leftovers
3 garlic cloves
1 heaped tsp tahini paste
A squirt of lemon juice
A glug of olive oil
Seasoning

I blitzed my leftover food adding the garlic cloves, tahini paste, lemon juice, olive oil, and seasoning.

And it tasted – and looked like – hummus!

We all love Bubble and Squeak made with our roast dinner leftovers. From being an economical way of using up our Sunday dinner surplus food, it's become one of our most popular dishes.

For a cold treat, do try a hummus variation. You'll be pleasantly surprised!

Fresh Vegetable Rainbow Roast

– Brighten-up Mealtime –

The seven colours of the rainbow are red, orange, yellow, green, blue, indigo, violet.

Do try this colourful dish of Rainbow Roast Vegetables. It's a great success whether you want to brighten up a family meal, or for entertaining!

Starting on the right, Cherry tomatoes, Carrot lengths, Yellow peppers, Asparagus, A Slice of Aubergine with the skin facing up, Red cabbage, in large chunks, slices of Red onions.

I tucked chopped onion underneath the vegetables, and added whole garlic cloves here and there, then neatened the arrangement.

Sprinkle with fresh herbs of your choice, drizzle with Olive Oil, cover with tinfoil and roast in the oven for about an hour, or until all the vegetables are soft.

Serve it on the table so everyone can see and admire it!

This recipe is ideal for vegetarians or vegans. Or you can add meat or fish to it.

I served it with Chicken Fricassee.

Of course you can change the vegetables, but keep the colours the same.

Chicken Fricassee is simply chopped onion, fried, then chopped chicken and mushrooms, served in a white sauce.

I added peas and sweetcorn.

Such a Waste of Food!

– Be Adventurous and Economical –

I bought some organic carrots in the supermarket. I'll gently cook the greenery for Sunday dinner and save some for tomorrow's stir-fry.

It's sad to think that probably everyone else who buys them will cut off the greenery and bin it.

The Koreans use all greenery from the top of veg, radishes, etc. and display them in bunches on their market stalls. Our farmers are throwing away a complete source of income every year. And you are possibly throwing away extra meals.

Like the Koreans, I now use kitchen scissors a lot. They're ideal for cutting up greens.

These fennel leaves are full of fennel flavour. You can add them to your cooking or mix them in a salad. But don't throw them away!

When I buy celery, I make sure that it has plenty of leaves inside it. They're my favourite bits for adding to cooking. I sometimes find chopped celery stalks too harsh for some recipes. The leaves are more delicate and taste much nicer.

Of course, I use the stalks in salads, or to chew on for a snack.

Here is one of the biggest food wastes of all.

Do you cut off all the greenery around a cauliflower and throw it away? Well don't do it again! You have at least one extra meal there!

Make a soup using any greenery recipe.

Cut the stalks into short lengths. Toss in olive oil and salt and roast for half an hour.

Do this when you have something else in the oven to save fuel.

Use the whole leaves, chopped finely, in a stir-fry.

The sprouted tops of onions are as strong as the onion bulb. They're sweeter and tastier.

And if the onion goes off, you can still use the tops.

Chop them up and use in a salad, or in any recipe that uses an onion.

And finally, beetroot.

The whole of a beetroot is edible and the leaves are full of goodness; Vitamins A, B6, C and D.

They also have iron, fibre, and bone-strengthening calcium.

Steam or saute the leaves, or juice them. Add a drop of water if necessary. It will be a beautiful green colour.

If all the vegetable leaves that you throw away in a year were piled up on your kitchen floor, you probably wouldn't be able to get in your kitchen!

So be more adventurous and economical and EAT YOUR GREENS!

Fried Green Tomatoes and Chutney

– Don't Waste Them! –

Fried Green Tomatoes

The first time I heard of Fried Green Tomatoes was when I watched the film Fried Green Tomatoes in the Whistle Stop Café. Then I got to eat them in BB King's restaurant in Beal Street, Memphis.

I make them every year now from the tomatoes grown in our garden and they're one of our favourite meals. And they're so easy.

1 egg, beaten

Flour

Oil

Slice the tomatoes. You'll probably get 4 slices per average-sized tomato.

Dip them in the beaten egg, and then into the flour, pressing them down to coat the slices well.

Fry them in hot, shallow oil, turning them over when crisp and golden.

The tomatoes will be crisp on the outside but juicy inside.

Lovely!

Green Tomato Chutney

Do prepare all your ingredients before you start cooking as it does take quite a long time to peel and chop everything.

You don't need to be completely accurate with the amounts. I topped up the green tomatoes with ripe ones. And as I didn't have marrow, I used pumpkin.

I used 10 jars. Traditionally you wash them and heat them in the oven to kill any germs or bacteria. I wash them by hand, then I wash them in the dishwasher.

3lb green tomatoes

1lb apples

1lb marrow

1lb onions
I used both brown and red onions

4oz dates, stoned

8oz sultanas
I used mixed fruit and less than 8oz

2lb soft brown sugar

1 tsp salt

¼ tsp cayenne pepper

1oz root ginger
I had ginger paste

1oz mustard seeds
I didn't have any so I used pickling spice

1pt malt vinegar

Peel and chop all vegetables and fruit. Place them all in a large saucepan and stir everything regularly.

The amount will reduce down.

Ready for potting up

Cook for around 2 hours, or longer if the vegetables are still hard and there's still a lot of liquid.

When it's thickened, leave to stand to cool slightly for a few minutes, then using a hand mixer, mix it up until smooth.

Pour it into jars. It will thicken as it cools, and it improves over the weeks. I got 10 jars!

Watermelon Suprises

– Five Recipes to Refresh –

Watermelon time is here again and the great green orbs are piled up in containers in the supermarkets as they take up a lot of space.

Do you use them all, or do you waste part of them?

I've never been a watermelon lover. I've always found them like solid water with big seeds in.

But now there seems to be a new type, with a lot more juicy flavour and tiny edible pips in them.

There are some delicious recipes for using watermelons and it's worth trying some of them.

Agua Fresca

This is a popular recipe from Mexico where it's sold everywhere.

Agua Fresca means Fresh Water.

4 cups of watermelon, chopped
I used about half of my large watermelon

½ cup lime juice

About 6 mint leaves

½ cup sugar

Approx ½ cup water

Blitz all the ingredients in a blender, then taste.

Add more sugar and water if needed.

Pour over ice cubes, and serve.

You can make this recipe with cucumbers, strawberries, or anything else that you fancy.

Melon and Ham

This is a popular starter. The contrasting flavours go together well.

Watermelon and Serrano Ham, as needed.

After slicing the ham, I cut it into bite-sized portions with kitchen scissors.

The next two recipes are made with watermelon peel.

To do this, cut off the watermelon, then use a sharp knife to slice off the thin outer green peel, and work with the inner peel, with a layer of watermelon on it. It's quite simple to do, but easier if you cut the watermelon into slices.

Candied Watermelon Peel

If you don't make anything else, you must try this one. It's absolutely delicious, and a good substitute for expensive candied fruit.

You can choose the best-shaped ones and put them in a nice box lined with greaseproof paper and give it as an unusual gift or keep it for Christmas– that is, if you can force yourself to leave any without eating them all!

Candying fruit or peel can be a long task, taking days. But this method only takes a few hours.

About 1lb (½kg) watermelon peel, sliced into squares, although the ends will be triangles.

Don't worry about the exact weight as if it weighs a bit more, it will all mix in.

1lb (12kg) sugar

12 fl oz (175ml) cold water

Put the peel in a pan, just cover with water and bring to the boil. Simmer for 10 minutes, drain, and cover with fresh water. Bring to the boil again and simmer for 20 minutes. Drain again.

Place the cooked peel in a bowl, cover with cold water and leave to soak for 24 hours, or overnight.

Drain the peel.

Place the sugar and water in a pan and bring to the boil, stirring with a wooden spoon until the sugar has dissolved.

Add the peel, then reduce the heat and simmer gently for 2-3 hours, or until the peel is translucent and most of the syrup has been absorbed.

Now you have two choices of what to do next.

You can spoon the peel into clean jars and cover with the syrup.

I raised the heat and gently boiled it until the syrup had started to crystallise.

You have to be very careful now, and stir the pan constantly to stop the syrup sticking.

It was ready in 50 minutes.

When it's all gone solid, spoon the peel onto a foil-covered dish, or on racks.

Spread out the pieces and leave to cool and dry out.

My recipe says you should place them in an oven on a very low heat, with the door open, for 10-12 hours, then sprinkle them with caster sugar. But mine were ready when they had cooled. And they didn't need caster sugar as they were coated in the crystallised syrup.

Pickled Watermelon Rind

All measurements are approximate as they don't really need to be accurate.

You can taste and add.

1lb (500g) watermelon rind

4 tbsp salt

2lb (1kg) sugar

1 pt (7ml) water

1¼ pint (750ml) white wine vinegar
I used cider vinegar

Small piece fresh ginger

1 tbsp allspice

1 tbsp cloves

2-3 strips orange or lemon peel
(I didn't bother)

Slice the watermelon rind into roughly 1 in cubes and place in a large bowl with the salt. Add enough water to cover and stir well until the salt has dissolved.

Cover with a cloth and leave to stand overnight.

The next day, drain the rind. Put in a pan and cover with fresh water. Bring to the boil, then reduce the heat and simmer for 15 minutes. Drain well.

Put the other ingredients in the rinsed-out pan. Bring to the boil and cook for about 5 minutes, stirring occasionally. Take out the spices. Add the rind and return to the boil, then reduce the heat and simmer on a medium heat for 45-60 minutes, until the rind is translucent.

Pack the mixture into clean jars and seal. The pickle will be ready to eat in about a month, although I found it delicious the next day!

My pickled syrup went quite thick and it's rather sweet, but tasty.

Watermelon Teabread

This is my original recipe and a great success.

Like all teabreads, the flavour improves daily for about a week, then it needs to be finished.

10oz (275g) plain flour, sifted

2 tsp bicarb of soda

A barely ½ tsp salt

1 tsp cinnamon

1 tsp ground ginger

4oz (115g) margarine

3 eggs

10oz (300g) sugar

About ¼ fresh watermelon
Check it as you don't want the mixture to be too runny and watery

Grease a 1lb loaf tin.

Preheat the oven to 180C/350F/gas mark 4.

Place all the ingredients in a food mixture or food processor, adding the eggs last.

Blend until smooth. Don't overmix it!

Pour into the loaf tin and bake for 50-60 minutes, until cooked when a skewer inserted into the centre comes out clean.

Leave to stand for 10 minutes, then turn out onto a plate to cool.

You can eat it with butter on, or just on its own.

Avocado Triplet

– Three Delicious Recipes –

Here are three tasty avocado recipes for you to try.

Avocado and Strawberry Milkshake

2 medium avocados
Approx 150g/½lb strawberries
Approx 200ml/½pint milk
Honey, to taste (1-2 tbsp)
Scoop of ice cream

Cut the avocado in half and gently remove the stone.

Scoop the flesh out of the avocado, using a teaspoon.

Place all the ingredients in the liquidiser and blitz.

Pour into glasses.

Guacamole

There are many versions of this Mexican dip. It's also a tasty salad ingredient.

This is my version.

2 medium avocados with the flesh scooped out

1 large soft tomato, chopped

1 small red onion, chopped

1 garlic clove, chopped finely

Lime juice

Olive oil

Seasoning

Squash the avocado to a paste using a fork.

Mix all the ingredients together and chill in the fridge until needed.

Spaghetti With Avocado Sauce

1 large avocado, flesh scooped out and mixed to a paste with a fork

2 garlic cloves, mashed finely

Olive oil

1 tbsp lemon juice

Large handful grated Parmesan

Large handful grated Cheddar, or cheese of your choice

2 finely chopped tomatoes

Splash of sweet chilli sauce or a sprinkling of chilli flakes

Seasoning

Pasta water to mix

Spaghetti for two

Cook the spaghetti.

Blend all the other ingredients in a food processor, then cook slowly in a saucepan until the onion's soft, adding some of the cooked spaghetti water to thin it down.

Serve the spaghetti with the avocado sauce over it.

Grate Parmesan on the top.

Natural Wines

– Make Your Own –

Returning to England after five years in Malta was a cultural shock.

Everything was so affordable there and all the alcohol was duty-free.

So my parents and other ex-pats started exchanging recipes and making their own wine and beer. It worked out even cheaper than the drinks in Malta!

I've brewed my own wine and beer for many years, and it used to be a popular hobby. But to my surprise I've watched a lot of the home-brew shops and suppliers go out of business.

I don't understand this, especially in these hard times when life is a financial struggle and alcohol is ridiculously expensive due to the tax that's charged per bottle.

My only cost is the sugar, and yeast with nutrients.

Vegetables like carrots, parsnips and potatoes are boiled, then the liquid is strained and the vegetables can be frozen and kept.

Yesterday I made lemon wine. It will be ready in time for the summer.

So how do you start?

You need a bucket, a couple of gallon jars, a plastic tube to remove the wine from the residue, bottles, and airlocks which go in the top of the gallon jars to keep any dirt out.

Here is a basic recipe for vegetable wines.

3kg/7lb parsnips

2 tsp citric acid/lemon juice

2 gallons water

1.5kg/3lb sugar

Yeast and nutrient

Pectic enzyme

Wash and dice the parsnips, then slice them and boil in 4 pints of water until tender, but not mushy.

Drain into the bucket and add 4 pints of cold water.

Add the sugar and citric acid and stir, then the yeast and nutrient when the water has cooled down.

Cover well and leave for 10 days, stirring every day.

Pour into a gallon jar, fit the airlock which has a dash of water in it, and leave to clear.

If a layer of sediment forms, rack into a clean gallon jar, top up again and leave until clear.

Place the plastic tube into the jar and suck the end to start the wine flowing into bottles.

Label, fit the top and store until wanted. Enjoy!

The best book ever written about home-made wine making is First Steps in Winemaking by C.J.J. Berry.

It's available online.

There are of course many other books, so do pick up any that you see around.

You can of course google the recipe of your choice. And you can buy any winemaking equipment online.

A selection of labels can be downloaded free of charge, which gives a professional finish to your bottles.

It's a great hobby because you never stop learning.

I love the way that you can make one batch of wine, spread into two gallon jars. And Mother Nature can turn both jars different colours with slightly different tastes.

So instead of paying a high price for a bottle of wine that you may not enjoy, why not make your own for a few pence?

And it's really handy if you wish to add more flavour to your cooking!

DELIGHTFUL

DESSERTS

Sussex Pond Pudding

- A Very Old Recipe -

The oldest recipe for Sussex Pond Pudding, called 'A Sussex Pudding', was in Hannah Woolley's 1670 book, 'The Queen-like Closet'. But obviously the recipe dated back a lot longer than that.

There was no mention of a lemon in the pudding in early recipes. Sometimes currants were included, but the butter was the most important ingredient.

Jane Grigson was the first known chef to write about including a whole lemon in her pudding, in her 1974 book, English Food.

I love cooking with suet because it always turns out successfully. (My fingers are crossed now!)

8oz self-raising flour

4oz suet

Approx. ¼ pint milk and water

4oz butter or margarine

4oz Demerara sugar
I didn't have any so I just used granulated sugar

1 large lemon

Sussex Pond Pudding is very easy to prepare, but it needs three hours of steaming. It's well worth the effort though! Just make sure that your saucepan doesn't boil dry.

Mix the flour and suet together in a bowl, then add the milk and water until it can be made into a dough. Let it stand for about ½ an hour, then roll it out, flouring the surface first.

Cut a quarter out of the rolled out dough, to use for the lid.

Butter a pudding basin that holds approx. 2½ pints. Lay the dough in the basin, pressing the edges together.

Place half the butter and sugar in the bowl.

Cut the top and bottom sticking-out bits off the lemon so it will stand upright. Prick it all over with a fork and stand it in the bowl.

Add the rest of the butter and sugar. Roll the rest of the dough into a circle to fit over the top of the bowl. Firmly press the edges together.

Grease a piece of greaseproof paper, fold a pleat in the middle and cover the top of the bowl.

Cover the whole bowl with tinfoil, again with a pleat in the middle to leave room if the dough rises.

Stand it in a saucepan, add boiling water and simmer for 3 hours, checking sometimes to make sure there's enough water in the saucepan.

Carefully lift the bowl out. Remove the tinfoil and greaseproof paper, and run a knife round inside the bowl to loosen the pudding.

Place a deep dish over the pudding and carefully turn the whole thing upside-down.

When cut, a 'pond' of liquid will run out.

The lemon will have become completely edible; skin and all. When you cut the pudding, do make sure that everyone gets a piece of the lemon.

Serve with custard or cream.

Rhubarb Buckle

– Dedicated to Laughton Village in Sussex –

Fruit Buckles are popular cakes in America.

As Laughton Village is known as The Village of the Buckle, I dedicate this recipe to them.

Apparently they're called a Buckle because the cake mix rises, then buckles under the weight of the fruit.

You can use any fruit in a Buckle. The Americans prefer a Blueberry Buckle, but any fruit will do.

I discovered this Rhubarb Buckle and I'll try strawberries in the Summer.

It's simple to make, but fiddly as there are three stages; the crumble topping, the fruit and the cake mix.

My advice is to assemble all the ingredients before you start.

For the crumble topping:

- 50g/2oz plain flour
- 50g/2oz sugar
- ½ tsp ground ginger
- 50g/2oz butter or margarine
- 25g/1oz oats
- Cling film

For the rhubarb:

- 225g/8oz rhubarb, cut into short lengths
- 50g/2oz sugar
- Zest 1 orange (optional)

For the cake:

- 120g/4oz butter or margarine
- 200g/7oz sugar
- Zest 1 orange
- 2 large eggs
- 200g/7oz plain flour
- 2 tsp baking powder
- 1 tsp vanilla
- 125ml/¼ pint soured cream
  I didn't have any so I used ½ cream and ½ yoghurt

Heat the oven to 180C/gas mark 4.

Grease a 20cm baking tin.

Measure out the topping ingredients in a bowl.

Mix it with your fingertips, then pat it into a ball. Wrap in clingfilm, squeezing it into a ball. Place in the fridge until needed.

In the same bowl, place all the fruit ingredients and stir until all the sugar sticks to the rhubarb.

Put all the cake ingredients except the eggs in a mixer or food processor. Mix for several minutes until smooth then add the eggs one at a time. Mix again.

Pour the cake mix into the tin.

Tip the rhubarb mix on top and spread the rhubarb pieces out evenly.

When you're ready to bake the cake, take the topping out of the fridge and pinch small pieces, dropping them evenly on top of the cake mix.

You're not covering the mixture with the topping as you do with a crumble. It will melt and spread during baking, giving a smooth, crisp topping.

Bake for approx. 1½ hours, checking towards the end to make sure the top doesn't burn.

Remove from the oven and let it cool for a ½ hour.

Place a plate over the baking tin after loosening the cake around the sides, then tip it upside-down onto the plate.

Now take another plate and tip it the right way up again.

Be careful as it is a crumbly cake and it might split.

Serve warm slices with custard or cream, or leave it to cool completely and serve slices.

It was even tastier the next day!

Kentish Cherry Batter Pudding

– Kentish Cherries. The Best! –

While driving along, we saw a sign beside the road saying English Cherries.

A few yards further on, we pulled into a layby where the cherries were being sold from a van.

In 43AD when the Romans arrived in Kent, they found wild cherries growing there. Later they imported the sweet, cultivated versions.

The Romans were given cherries as part of their rations. And the number of cherry trees is blamed on the Romans spitting out the stones.

Kent is known as the Garden of England and produces most of the country's cherries throughout the Summer.

At the start of the 20th century Kent had more than 5,000 cherry orchards. By the end of the century there were less than 600. But the good news is planting is increasing every year. The Kentish cherries are making a comeback!

3 tbsp Kirsch or Cherry Brandy
I didn't have any, so I used Sherry

450g/1lb pitted cherries
You don't have to be exactly accurate with the weight

50g/2oz plain flour

50g/2oz caster sugar
I didn't have any so I used granulated sugar

2 eggs, separated

300ml/½ pint milk

75g/3oz melted butter

Sprinkle the kirsch over the cherries. Leave them to soak for about 30 minutes, turning them in the juice a few times. Mix the flour and sugar together, then slowly stir in the egg yolks and milk until it becomes a smooth batter. Add half the melted butter. Let stand for 30 minutes.

Heat the oven to 220C/425F/gas mark 7.

Pour the remaining butter into a 600ml/pint dish and spread it round the sides.

Put it in the oven to heat.

Whisk the egg whites until stiff, then gently fold them into the batter with the cherries and kirsch.

Pour the mixture into the baking dish and bake for approx. 15 minutes, then turn down the heat to 180C/350F/gas mark 4. Bake for a further 20 minutes, until golden and set in the centre.

It will still have a slight wobble.

Serve hot either on its own or with custard, cream or ice-cream. It's also nice served cold the following day.

Sussex Ripe Tart

– A Celebration of the Cherry Harvest –

The Sussex village of Ripe used to have cherry trees, which have all long gone.

I'd heard about this recipe but I had trouble finding it. I assume that it's hundreds of years old.

It was made when a pie feast celebrated the cherry harvest, probably in July.

These are the pastry ingredients, but I used ready made puff pastry. And you could use shortcrust.

8oz plain flour

Pinch of salt

1oz cornflour

2 tsp icing sugar

4oz butter

1 egg yolk

2 tbsp cold water

Mix ingredients together.

Knead lightly.

Leave in fridge for ½ hour.

Line a 9-inch flan tin. Prick the pastry all over with a fork or use baking beans. Bake blind at 200C/gas mark 6 for 10-15 minutes.

For the Filling:

1lb cherries, stoned

2 eggs

3oz ground almonds

Few drops of almond essence (optional)

4oz icing sugar

Fill the pastry case with the stoned cherries. Gently press them into the pastry.

My neighbour lent me her amazing cherry stoner gadget.

Mix the icing sugar, eggs, ground almonds, almond essence (if using).

Pour the mixture over the cherries.

Bake at 170C/gas mark 3 for 40-50 minutes, until golden on the top.

Serve it hot or cold, with cream or a scoop of ice cream if you like.

The top goes slightly crusty like a meringue.

Note that there's no sugar in this tart, just icing sugar, and the sweetness of the cherries.

I bought my cherries by the roadside from a Kent farm which I've since visited.

Kentish Gypsy Tart

– A Fruit and Hop Picking Favourite –

This simple sweet tart probably got its name from the Gypsies who used to travel to Kent to help with the fruit and hop picking.

It was also a popular dessert with school dinners.

If you don't want to make the pastry yourself for the base, use ready-made pastry from a supermarket.

They are very good and they save you a lot of time.

Shortcrust pastry

1 tin of evaporated milk, chilled overnight in the fridge

225g/10oz soft, dark brown muscovado sugar
I used granulated sugar as I didn't have any brown, and I couldn't quite get rid of the grainy taste, no matter how long I beat it for. It was still tasty, but slightly grainy

Pre-heat the oven to 200C/400F/gas mark 6.

Grease a flan dish 25cm/10ins diameter.

Roll out your pastry and line the dish with it.

I don't use baking beads. I Just prick it all over with a fork.

Bake it for 10-15 minutes. Remove it. Leave it to cool.

Whisk together the evaporated milk and sugar on full power for 12-15 minutes until the mixture becomes light, fluffy, and coffee coloured.

Pour the mixture into the cooled base and bake in the oven for 10 minutes.

Remove from the oven and leave the tart to get cold.

This is delicious but very rich, so serve small slices.

Sussex Pumpkin Tart

– It Does Taste Good! –

The Americans love their Pumpkin Pies. But they're not pies as they don't have a lid. And I can't understand why they often use tinned pumpkin when they have a wide variety of pumpkins grown there.

Here is my recipe using pumpkin from a local pumpkin farm. It's very easy to make.

Roast the pumpkin whole in the oven for 1-1½ hours until the skin is soft when you poke it.

Cut the pumpkin into four when it's cool enough to handle. Scoop out the pips and pith with a spoon and peel the skin off.

Pastry for the base:

I bought supermarket puff pastry. It's good and reasonably low-priced. You could use shortcrust.

24oz cooked pumpkin

4oz brown sugar

⅛ tsp salt

1½ tsps ground cinnamon

½ tsp ground ginger

¼ tsp ground cloves

3 eggs

10 fl oz single cream

Preheat oven to 190C/375F/gas mark 5.

In a large bowl and using an electric hand mixer, or place in a mixer, puree the pumpkin.

Add the other ingredients, adding the cream last, and mix everything together.

Roll out the pastry and line a flan dish.

Tip the mixture on top of the pastry and bake in the oven for approx 50 minutes, until brown on the top.

Remove from the oven and leave it to cool and to set more.

Serve with single cream, for flavour and to give it some colour. Or add your own garnish ideas, like a sprig of mint, or some strawberry slices.

It's not the prettiest dessert that I've made, but it does taste good!

Pumpkin and Apple Pie

– A Classic Pie with a Twist –

I've made Pumpkin Pie several times and the Americans love it but I've found it too bland and tasteless.

I decided to have one last try as I had a glut of pumpkins and apples.

12oz cooked pumpkin

4oz cooked apple

2 eggs

4oz sugar, whatever is available

4 tbsp honey

1½tsp cinnamon

1 tsp ground ginger

¼ tsp cloves

½ tsp salt

For the pastry, I used a packet of ready rolled shortcrust, which I rolled out even thinner.

Butter a pie dish and line the pastry in it.

I had enough for two dishes. I gave one pie to my neighbour.

Blitz all the ingredients together and pour into the dishes.

Shake a thin layer of sugar over the top and bake for up to an hour until the filling begins to solidify.

Serve in slices, with cream in you like.

Apple Cheesecake

– With Sussex Slipcote Cheese –

Sussex Slipcote is a fresh cheese usually made from ewes' milk by the High Weald Dairy in West Sussex, England. The cheese is usually round in shape with a very soft creamy texture.

There are two different explanations given for the meaning of "Slipcote". The dairy explains that "'Slipcote' is an old English word meaning little (slip) piece of cottage (cote) cheese". Another explanation is that "Slipcote" describes the cheese's tendency to slip out of its rind while maturing. Sussex Slipcote has been made in England since the Middle Ages.

For the base:

275g broken biscuits

1 tsp cinnamon

125g butter or margarine

1 tbsp runny honey

For the filling:

200g apples, preferably cookers, peeled and chopped

1 tbsp lemon juice

150g sugar

400g soft cheese
I used 1 round of Sussex Slipcote soft cheese

300ml double cream

Use a small amount of the butter to grease a 23cm round baking dish.

Place the biscuits in a small carrier bag and crush them with a rolling-pin.

You don't need to crush them to fine crumbs. Leave some slightly larger pieces to add an interesting texture.

Melt the butter over a low heat. When it melts, turn off the heat and stir in the biscuit crumbs.

Add the cinnamon and the honey, stirring well.

Tip them into the dish, spread them out and flatten them, using the back of a spoon and pushing them up the sides of the dish.

Put the apples in a small saucepan with the lemon juice and 25g of sugar.Cook slowly, stirring, until the apples have turned to a pulp. Leave to cool.

The apples were freshly picked off our neighbours' tree.

Beat the cheese, cream and remaining sugar in a bowl with an electric whisk until soft peaks are formed.

Gently fold in the apple.

Tip the mixture on top of the biscuit base.

Leave it in the fridge to set.

Strawberry Slipcote Sweet

– A Delicious Recipe –

This is a simple, delicious dessert, using the High Weald Dairy Sussex Slipcote soft cheese.

1 strawberry jelly
2 High Weald Dairy Sussex Slipcote soft cheese
1 small punnet of English strawberries
Sugar

Prepare the strawberries. Wash them, slice into a bowl and shake some sugar over them.

Make the jelly. Cool it slightly.

Beat the Sussex Slipcote cheeses until they're mixed, then stir them into the jelly.

Add the strawberries. Mix.

Leave to set in the fridge.

The Original 'Hungry Monk' Banoffi Pie

– And The True History –

Banoffee Pie, originally spelt Banoffi Pie, has become one of the most popular sweets in the world.

I heard that it was a favourite of Elvis Presley. And I've also heard it described as an American dish!

Well no it's not. It was created in the small village of Jevington, near Eastbourne, in Sussex in 1971.

I was given the recipe by a chef friend in 1976. The original recipe (see below) had coffee in it.

My chef friend used Camp Coffee, the liquid coffee in a bottle.

I don't add any coffee.

The restaurant where it was created is now closed. It is a 16th century building which was originally a monk's rest.

It was bought and modernised by Nigel and Sue Mackenzie, and then they set to work with their chef Ian Dowding to create a menu of original dishes.

They needed one more dessert and they experimented with different fruits. But none of them were quite right, until they tried bananas. And Banoffi Pie was born!

Nigel named it Signor Banoffi's Pie, to make it sound Italian.

Customers from as far away as London called to book a table, first checking that the Banoffi Pie was still on the menu.

The restaurant was fully booked for months ahead.

It was said that David Essex went there after his performance on the theatre stage in Eastbourne and he was told that the restaurant closed at 10.

'But don't you know who I am?' poor David desperately asked.

'Yes sir, but we close at 10,' was the rather heartless reply.

I'm a firm believer that it's a restaurant's duty to feed a hungry customer and they should be able to put something together, like a salad or a sandwich.

The recipe for Banoffi Pie has never been a secret. It was published in the Hungry Monk's cookery book in 1974, The Deeper Secrets of the Hungry Monk, which sold over 100,000 copies.

Nestle printed the recipe on the side of their condensed milk tins.

Recipe courtesy of Ian Dowding of 'The Hungry Monk'

Serves 8-10

For the pastry:

- 9oz plain flour
- 1oz icing sugar
- 4½ oz butter
- 1 egg and 1 egg yolk

For the Banoffi toffee sauce:

- 1½ tins condensed milk – 13.5oz each
- 5-6 firm yet ripe bananas
- 1½ cups double cream – whipping cream or crème fraîche work well too
- 1 tsp instant coffee
- 1 tbsp caster sugar
- 1 tsp freshly ground coffee

For the pastry, place the flour and sugar in a bowl, cut the butter into cubes and then rub the mixture together until it resembles fine bread crumbs. Work the egg into the dough to form a paste, then cover and chill for half an hour. Preheat the oven to 400°F.

When ready, lightly grease a 10-inch x 1½-inch deep loose bottomed tart tin, and line with the pastry thinly rolled out. Prick the base all over with a fork, line with parchment paper and weigh down with dry beans. Bake for 15 minutes then remove the beans and parchment. Put the pastry case back into the oven and cook until its evenly golden. Remove from the oven and cool.

For the toffee sauce, start by placing the unopened tins in a deep pot, cover with water, and bring to a boil on the stovetop. Cover with a lid and transfer to a preheated 285°F oven for 3½ hours. Lift the tins from the water and allow to cool completely before opening. Note: The longer they cook, the darker and thicker the toffee will be.

To compose the pie, carefully spread the toffee over the cooked pastry, then top with peeled and sliced bananas. Whip the cream, sugar and instant coffee granules, until thick and smooth. To finish, spoon the cream over the bananas, up to the edge of the pastry, then lightly sprinkle with freshly ground coffee, and garnish with some sliced bananas on top, just before serving.

COOK'S NOTE: The caramel-toffee sauce is a great addition to many dishes such as ice-cream and poached pears.

I usually now use a cheesecake base, with crushed biscuits stirred into melted butter and a tablespoon of Golden Syrup, then pressed into a pie dish. Pour in the caramel sauce, cover it with slices of banana and top it with double cream.

Nestle now produces a caramel version of their condensed milk, so you don't need to boil the cans for three hours.

Mary Berry's Banoffee Pie has a simple way to make the Caramel Sauce.

Heat 3oz butter and 3oz sugar in a pan and stir over a low heat. Add the contents of a tin of condensed milk and bring to a boil, stirring continuously until it turns a dark golden. Add a teaspoonful of vanilla essence, stir, and tip over the base in the pie dish.

This tastes almost the same as the boiled condensed milk and is much simpler to make.

Michael Terence
Publishing
www.mtp.agency

mtp.agency

@mtp_agency

Printed in Dunstable, United Kingdom

66335247R00070